92
W

REACHING FOR THE STARS

HEATHER WHITESTONE
Miss America with a Mission

Jill C. Wheeler

Published by Abdo & Daughters, 4940 Viking Drive, Suite 622, Edina, Minnesota 55435.

Copyright © 1996 by Abdo Consulting Group, Inc., Pentagon Tower, P.O. Box 36036, Minneapolis, Minnesota 55435 USA. International copyrights reserved in all countries. No part of this book may be reproduced in any form without written permission from the publisher.

Printed in the United States.

Cover Photo credit: Bettmann Archives
Interior Photo credits: Wide World Photos

Edited by Rosemary Wallner

Library of Congress Cataloging-in-Publication Data

Wheeler, Jill C., 1964
Heather Whitestone—Miss America with a Mission / Jill C. Wheeler.
  p. cm. — (Reaching for the stars)
Summary: Traces the life of the hearing-impaired woman who became the first Miss America with a disability.
        ISBN 1-56239-499-1
1. Whitestone, Heather—Juvenile literature. 2. Beauty contestants—United States—Biography—Juvenile literature. 3. Women, Deaf—United States—Biography—Juvenile literature. 4. Miss American Pageant, Atlantic City, N.J.—Juvenile literature. [1. Whitestone, Heather. 2. Beauty contestants. 3. Deaf. 4. Women—Biography.] I. Title. II. Series.
HQ1220.U5W44 1995
791.6'2—dc20
[B]   95-17422
                                                                    CIP
                                                                     AC

TABLE OF CONTENTS

A DREAM COME TRUE

It was the moment the 51 contestants had looked forward to. The annual Miss America pageant was drawing to a close. Co-host Regis Philbin was ready to name the first runner-up. The remaining contestant would be Miss America 1994.

"And the first runner-up," said the co-host, "is…Miss Virginia!"

Miss Alabama, Heather Whitestone, became the last contestant. She didn't know she had won. Then Miss Virginia, Cullen Johnson, pointed to her. "You won! You won!" Cullen said. Suddenly, Heather realized what had happened. She burst into happy tears as the crown was placed on her head.

Still smiling and crying, Heather took a victory stroll down the runway. She held up her hand as she walked down the runway. She flashed the American Sign Language gesture for "I Love You." The crowd clapped and shouted.

But Heather Whitestone couldn't hear the excited crowd. Heather is hearing impaired. The 21-year-old woman was the first person with a disability to win the Miss America pageant.

Miss Alabama, Heather Whitestone, wins the 1994 Miss America contest. She didn't know she had won. Then Miss Virginia, Cullen Johnson, pointed to her and said, "You won! You won!"

GROWING UP IN SILENCE

When Heather was born, she could hear. She became sick, however, when she was 18 months old and lost most of her hearing. She couldn't hear at all in her right ear. She could hear only 5 percent of sounds in her left ear. Today, she wears a hearing aid in that ear. Even with the hearing aid, she can hear very little. "I don't remember what it was like to be a hearing person," she said. "I was just a baby."

Heather grew up in Dothan, Alabama. She was the youngest of three girls. Her father owned a furniture store. When Heather's parents realized their daughter couldn't hear, they had to make a decision. They knew that many people who are hearing impaired learn to communicate with American Sign Language. They use hand gestures in place of words. Other people who are hearing impaired learn to speak. Heather's mother, Daphne Gray, made the decision. Heather would learn to speak.

Heather wanted to be like other people. Her mother remembered her young daughter's strong will.

"Before we started teaching her to sign, she was trying to learn to talk," said Daphne. "When we started the signs, she went mute on me."

Daphne thought speaking would be important. She didn't think Heather could lead a normal life without it. "I don't know how many people know sign language," Daphne said. "But I'm willing to bet it is very, very few."

Heather credits her mother with many of her abilities. "She gave me strength to face all my problems," Heather said. "The word 'impossible' is not in her vocabulary. She made me learn to speak when I was little so I could live a normal life."

MY NAME IS...

Learning to talk was very hard for Heather. She could barely hear words. Her mother helped her. "I did a lot of her training sitting behind her back," Daphne recalled. "I would sit behind her so she couldn't see my lips. I'd say, 'What is your name?' She really had to use what little hearing she had." Heather said English is the hardest language for deaf people to learn.

"When I was little, it was so hard to pronounce words," she remembered. "Sometimes I felt so lonely because I couldn't communicate. It took me six years to say my last name correctly."

When Heather was five years old, she began dance lessons. Her mother wanted Heather to learn to dance. She thought it would help her speak. "When you feel the vibrations of music," Heather explained, "you can hear high and low pitches." Daphne told Heather the high and low pitches were the same when people spoke.

Heather loved to dance and developed a love of ballet. She also loved classical and Christian music. She could hear a little of the music, but no words.

Heather loved to dance and developed a love of ballet.

WORKING HARD AT SCHOOL

Heather attended public schools in her hometown until she was 11 years old. Then she went to the Central Institute for the Deaf. It was a private school in St. Louis, Missouri. At the school, Heather took classes to learn to speak and read English. She also learned American Sign Language. And she learned to read lips. Reading lips means watching people's lips when they speak. People can discover what others are saying by watching their lips.

Heather spent three years at that school. Then she moved on. "At Central, they require graduates to go to public school," Heather said. "That's so they can become a citizen of the world, not just a citizen of the deaf world. I support that."

Heather enrolled in Northview High School in her hometown. Then her parents divorced. Heather moved to Birmingham with her mother.

She spent her sophomore year at the Alabama School of Fine Arts in Birmingham. She studied ballet. But the school was near a busy freeway. Many of the cars and trucks used CB

Academy Award-winning actress Marlee Matlin, left, uses sign language as she converses with newly crowned Miss America, Heather Whitestone. They met at the National Easter Seal Awards ceremony, October 18, 1994.

radios. Heather's hearing aid picked up signals from these radios. It was hard for Heather to concentrate. In class, she kept hearing the radios.

The next year, she changed schools again. She was sad to leave her ballet classes. Yet she knew other classes were important, too. She wanted her high school life to be more like other people's. At Berry High School, she found that life. She worked with a special education teacher. She talked, read lips, and took her own notes in class. She graduated with honors in 1991.

After graduation, Heather wanted to spend more time with other people who were hearing impaired. "I thought I would be so much happier in a deaf world," she said. She entered the Miss Deaf Alabama Contest. That experience taught her something.

Most people who are hearing impaired talk to each other through sign language. Heather thought sign language restricted these people. "I realized sign language puts more limits to their dreams," she said. "Which is very sad. It's very hard to communicate between hearing and deaf people."

College was Heather's next challenge. At first, she had trouble. The college wouldn't give her a sign language interpreter. She could read lips, yet she still missed parts of class lectures. Some of her teachers helped her. They wrote down their lecture notes and gave her copies. She studied these notes late into the night.

Eventually, Heather changed colleges. She enrolled at Jacksonville State University. She wanted to study accounting and dance. The university gave her interpreters to help with her classes.

Heather needed extra money to pay her expenses. She decided to compete in beauty pageants. She knew people who entered beauty pageants could win money and scholarships.

A VISIT TO ATLANTIC CITY

The Miss America Pageant is the biggest beauty pageant of all. It is held each year in Atlantic City, New Jersey. To compete, contestants must first win their state pageants.

In 1993, Heather entered the Miss Alabama contest. She became first runner-up. As runner-up, she couldn't compete in the contest. That didn't stop her from traveling to New Jersey. She wanted to see the pageant and went there with her mother. They cheered for Miss Alabama 1993.

Late one night after the pageant, Heather and her mother visited the Atlantic City Convention Center. The center is where the contest had been held. Heather walked down the famous runway. The 1993 Miss America had walked down that runway the night before. Heather told her mother, "This is what I want to do."

"I realized that Miss America had a world of opportunity," Heather said. "She could make a big difference. She could reach other people's lives. I wanted that opportunity."

Former Miss America Phyllis George (1971), left, and Kaye Lani Rae Rafko (1988), right, sit with Heather Whitestone. They are at the ceremony to launch the 75th anniversary of the Miss America Organization.

Heather entered the Miss Alabama competition again in June 1994. She performed a ballet dance for the talent competition. She remembered it was hard to hear the music. "All I could hear was clapping," she said. "I didn't want to hear clapping. I wanted to hear my music." In spite of her trouble, she won the pageant and was crowned Miss Alabama 1994. She was going to the Miss America pageant.

LOOK AT ME, NOT MY DISABILITY

Before the pageant, Heather gave an interview. "I know I'll get attention because of my deafness," she told a reporter. "I don't want that, but it's going to happen anyway.

"When I walk into the interview, I'll make sure they see who and what I am," she continued. "Not just my deafness. I think I have a good chance. Not because of my deafness. No. Erase that. I have a good attitude and am a positive role model. I know I can be Miss America."

Heather Whitestone signs as she holds her first news conference at the TropWorld Casino Resort, September 18, 1994, after becoming Miss America.

Heather Whitestone shares a laugh with Senator Howell Heflin of Alabama during a visit with the Alabama Congressional delegation on Capitol Hill.

A company that makes hearing aids helped Heather. The company discovered that Heather couldn't hear her music during the Miss Alabama Pageant. They gave her a new hearing aid. It helped stop background noises. Not hearing background noise would help Heather focus on the music.

Heather met the other contestants at Walt Disney World on Labor Day weekend. Next, the contestants traveled to Philadelphia, Pennsylvania. They toured the city. Finally, they arrived in Atlantic City. They began rehearsing for the pageant.

Before the pageant, Heather recalled what others had said about her when she was young. Many people had said she would never be able to speak or dance. Yet her mother always said she could. "I looked at how my mother fought for me to achieve my dreams," Heather said. "And then I looked at where I was. And I would start to cry."

WINNING HEARTS AND POINTS

Judges compare the Miss America contestants in several areas. One is the swimsuit competition. Another is the evening gown competition. There is also a talent competition. This preliminary competition lasts two weeks. Heather won the swimsuit and talent events.

When the preliminary competition ended, the judges selected ten semi-finalists. Heather was chosen as a semi-finalist. The judges then narrowed their choice to five finalists. Heather was among them. The finalists again performed their talent routines. People watching the pageant on TV saw these finalists perform.

Heather delighted the judges with her talent routine. She performed a 2 1/2-minute classical ballet dance. She danced to the song, "Via Dolorosa." The audience went wild. They gave her four standing ovations.

Kathie Lee Gifford, the pageant co-host, loved Heather's dance. "I was just so moved by the human spirit," she said later.

Miss America, Heather Whitestone, (right), joins eight former title holders as they blow out candles on a cake, launching the 75th anniversary of the Miss America Organization.

Heather Whitestone (second from right) and television personality Willard Scott (right) pose for cameras with actor and actress Pam Dawber and Mark Harmon during the Hero Awards gala, September 26, 1994.

Heather surprised many people with her dance. They asked her how she could dance if she couldn't hear the music. Heather told them that she counts the beats of the music in her head. She moves in time to those beats. She matches her moves to the pitch of the music.

In the last part of the pageant, the finalists answered questions. Regis Philbin asked Heather a question, too. He asked her how she would motivate youth.

She could barely hear the question. Yet she answered him out loud. "My good attitude helped me get through hard times and believe in myself," she said. After that last pageant event, the judges added up the points. Heather was announced the winner.

After the pageant, the new Miss America met with reporters. Heather asked the reporters to face her directly. She also asked them to speak slowly. When she had trouble understanding one reporter's question, she asked the other reporters to stop taking photographs. "You keep flashing," she said. "It's hard for me to see his lips."

She told the reporters about answering the interview questions. "The most difficult obstacle [of the pageant] was the interview competition," she said. "I had to let [the co-hosts] know they had to speak slowly. If they looked at me directly, everything would be all right."

Heather won more than a crown at the pageant. She received a new car. She also received a $35,000 scholarship. Her dream had come true.

HERE SHE IS…MISS AMERICA

After the pageant, Heather became very busy. She appeared on TV shows. She spoke to many groups. Many reporters interviewed her.

She also traveled to Washington, D.C., where she met with a special group of people. The people represented other people with disabilities. The group shared stories. They talked about how life is more difficult for people with disabilities. Heather had her own stories to share. She gave the group some advice. Focus on what you can do, she said, not what you can't do.

Here she is, Miss America—Heather Whitestone.

"I never thought of myself as disabled," she told them.

Heather talked about her views on how people who are hearing impaired should communicate. Heather said she would rather speak than use sign language. She believes speaking is better. She said sign language limits people who are hearing impaired. "As long as they don't use English, it's not going to help them be successful," she said.

Heather's views support mainstreaming. Mainstreaming is putting people with disabilities and people without disabilities together. There are many advantages to mainstreaming. People with disabilities don't feel left out. People without disabilities learn more about others who live with a disability.

Not everyone agrees with Heather's views. Some people think that people with disabilities, including people who are hearing impaired, should have their own culture. That way, they can share experiences and support each other. "I don't think [Heather] is really deaf," said one student who is hearing impaired. "She's more a part of the hearing world."

Heather understands how both sides feel. She wants to bridge this gap during her reign. She also wants both sides to succeed.

Heather has a special way of encouraging people to succeed. She calls it STAR. It stands for Success Through Action and Realization. "The program has five steps, just like a star has five points," Heather explained.

The first step is to have a positive attitude. The second step is to believe in your dreams. The third is to be willing to work hard. "I don't believe success just happens," Heather said. "You have to plan to make it happen. It takes time."

The fourth step is to face your obstacles. Heather likes to quote her role model, Helen Keller. Like Heather, Helen was hearing impaired. She was also seeing impaired. Helen Keller said, "Know your problems, but don't let them master you. Let them teach you patience, sweetness, and kindness. Because you never know what miracles you will bring in other people's lives. Or your life."

The final step is to have a support team. "I tell the children that everybody needs support," Heather said. "It's so easy to give up if you do it on your own. But so many times, famous people have failed before their dreams eventually came true. So many young people don't realize that.

"Children already have their team started," she added. "They have their parents, their teachers, their principal, their friends, and God."

One Birmingham school already is using Heather's STAR program. Heather hopes other young people will hear about it. She hopes the program will help them as it helped her. "I want deaf people to know there are no limits to who you are," she said. "Hearing and deaf people have so much to offer each other. I want to build bridges between us."

Heather helps out at her college as a counselor for students who are hearing impaired. She is also a member of the Alabama Governor's Task Force for the Deaf and Hard of Hearing. She has thought about becoming a teacher like her mother. "Maybe I'll be a math teacher or a counselor," she said, "so that I could see young people every day."

A MESSAGE OF MOTIVATION

"I really believe the most handicapped person in the world is a negative thinker," Heather said. "I want to send a message. I believe that positive thinking is the solution to this problem." Heather reminds people of what her mother told her: The last letters of "American" spell, "I can."

As Miss America, Heather traveled thousands of miles. She delivered many speeches to young people around the nation. Her platform was "Youth Motivation: Anything Is Possible."

Heather hoped to convince young people they have the power to realize their dreams. "When children see me speaking and see me dance, they will realize they have no excuse for not making their own dreams come true."

Heather Whitestone.

Heather realized she had a tough job. There are many kinds of disabilities. People who have disabilities face different challenges. People who don't have disabilities can help. They must support people with disabilities. They must try to understand special needs. They must realize everyone has some kind of disability.

"I tell young children with disabilities that they are not the only ones who have handicaps," she said. "Every one of us on this Earth has handicaps…. Once you overcome the bad attitude, you'll overcome anything."

"So many young people have problems they have to face," she continued. "Most of the time, they just give up. I want to challenge them to make their dreams come true."

After her reign, Heather has plans for her life. She wants to become a dance teacher. She wants to graduate from Jacksonville State University. She also has a dream of living by the ocean someday.

Knowing Heather Whitestone, those dreams will come true as well.

GLOSSARY

American Sign Language—a way of communicating using hand signs instead of words and phrases.

Hearing Impaired—someone who has problems with their hearing.

Interpreter—a person who helps others understand the meaning of words.

Mainstreaming—putting people with disabilities in the same classrooms as people without disabilities.

Mute—unable to talk.

Scholarship—money given to a student to attend a school.

Standing Ovation—When people in a theatre, auditorium, stadium, etc., rise to their feet and applaude for a performer or speaker.